Growing Bulbs

WRITER

PEGGY HENRY

PHOTOGRAPHER

SAXON HOLT

AVON BOOKS ◆ NEW YORK

Product Manager: CYNTHIA FOLLAND, NK LAWN & GARDEN CO.

Acquisition, Development and Production Services: JENNINGS & KEEFE: Media Development, Corte Madera, CA

Acquisition: JACK JENNINGS, BOB DOLEZAL

Series Concept: BOB DOLEZAL

Project Director: JILL FOX

Developmental Editor: CYNTHIA PUTNAM

Horticultural Consultant: RG TURNER JR

Photographic Director: SAXON HOLT

Art Director (interior): BRAD GREENE

Cover Designer: KAREN EMERSON

Page Make-up: BRAD GREENE

Illustrator: JAMES BALKOVEK

Copy Editor: VIRGINIA RICH

Proofreader: LYNN FERAR

Indexer: SYLVIA COATES

Photo Assistant: PEGGY HENRY

Additional Photographers: Pages 6-7 (background) and 27 (Double-Digging) Alan Copeland and Barry Shapiro; pages 32-33 (Botrytis, Borers, Thrips and Viruses) Margery Daughtrey; pages 54 (Amaryllis), 57 (Cape hyacinth), 59 (Foxtail lily), 61 (Glory-of-the-snow), 65 (Candidum hybrids), 70 (Puschkinia and Snowdrop), 71 (Squill) and 75 (Winter aconite) Netherlands Flowerbulb Information Center; pages 67 (Montbretia) and 71 (Spider lily) Charles Cresson

Color Separations: PREPRESS ASSEMBLY INCORPORATED

Printing and Binding: WOLFER PRINTING COMPANY

PRINTED IN THE USA

Cover: Perky, candy-stripped tulips provide early spring color along an entrance path.

First Avon Books Trade Printing: February 1995

ISBN: 0-380-77428-3

Library of Congress Cataloging-in-Publication Number: 94-96453

Special thanks to: Brookside Botanic Garden, Montgomery, MD; Valerie Brown; Theo Crawford; Margery Daughtrey, Cornell University, Ithaca, NY; Dan Davids, Davids & Royston Bulbs, Gardena, CA; Phil Edinger; Sally Ferguson, Netherlands Flowerbulb Information Center; Filoli Gardens, Woodside, CA; Peggy Henry; Longwood Gardens, Kennett Square, PA; Star MacKay; Dorothy Orr; Beth Records; Wayne Roderick; Diana Stratton; Katie Trefethen; Debbie Van Bourgondlen, Van Bourgondlen Bulbs, Babylon, NY

AVON BOOKS
A division of
The Hearst Corporation
1350 Avenue of the Americas
New York, New York 10019

AVON TRADEMARK REG. U.S. PAT. OFF.
AND IN OTHER COUNTRIES, MARCA
REGISTRADA, HECHO EN U.S.A.

TABLE OF CONTENTS

ENJOYING BULBS

WHY GROW BULBS?

Planting a bulb is like hiding a secret treasure. You bury it in the ground, see nothing for months and often forget all about it. Then one day a small green sprout appears, signaling the arrival of a new season. The sprout matures into a wonderful flower of any imaginable color, blooms radiantly and then slowly retreats underground into dormancy until the cycle begins again the following season.

Bulbs are unique in the flower garden. They require very little care and yet produce some of the showiest flowers in nature. There are bulbs that thrive in the coldest or the warmest of climates. Unlike perennials, they need little or no pruning, staking or transplanting, and unlike annuals, most come back every year. They take up little space and can enliven any garden.

Most bulbs bloom in the spring, and many people think of flowering bulbs as a sign of spring, but there are bulbs that bloom in every season of the year. Winter aconite, *Eranthis hyemalis,* grows right up through the snow in late winter or early spring, exploding with bright yellow blossoms that resemble buttercups and carry a sweet, honey fragrance. There are many summer-blooming bulbs and quite a few fall-blooming bulbs as well. Although they may be less noticeable than spring bulbs because of the other plants flowering around them, they too can be added to many gardens for nearly year-round bulb beauty.

BULBS IN NATURE

Knowing the origin of a bulb gives you clues to its requirements. Of the bulbs we grow today, many of the spring-flowering bulbs originated in the Mediterranean region, from Spain and North Africa across into Turkey, and in Iran and western China. Those regions have wet winters and hot, dry summers, so the bulbs have adapted by beginning growth in winter and flowering in the cool, wet spring. During its growing period, the plant stores food in the underground bulb, and then, as summer heat and drought approach, the plant dies back.

Summer-flowering bulbs typically come from parts of Africa where the wet and dry cycles are different from those of the Mediterranean region. The rain occurs in the hot months, and the winters are cool and dry. Bulbs from this area go dormant in the winter and sprout in response to moisture in the spring. By summer, they are in bloom.

The popularity of bulbs over the centuries has invariably meant that the plants were collected from the wild. This practice has led to the extinction of certain species and near extinction for many others. It is important to buy bulbs from reputable companies that do not collect from the wild—a practice that is illegal in many places. There are more than enough types of bulbs already in cultivation to meet market demands and to further the development of new varieties.

To many people, bulbs in flower—especially lively yellow tulips—mean spring has sprung.

5

FIVE BULB GARDENS

There are many ways to use bulbs in your garden. Choosing a plan that suits your landscape and life-style is the first step in bulb gardening. Here are a few classic examples to stimulate your imagination when planning your garden.

It takes a good understanding of timing and design to execute a flower garden composed entirely of bulbs successfully.

A mixed flower bed combines annuals, perennials and bulbs, and can even include shrubs and small trees.

Outdoor container gardens with bulbs are easy to plant and care for. You can plant annuals right over the bulbs after the bulbs have died back.

Bulbs forced to bloom out of season for indoor placement can be enjoyed like arrangements of cut flowers, but have a longer life.

Naturalized plantings are designed to look as though they occurred on their own. Plant bulbs in an open space where they will multiply for many years.

TYPES OF BULBS

All bulbs have an enlarged stem or root that increases their capacity for storage. Each type is uniquely adapted to store food for relatively long periods of dormancy so that it can grow and bloom when conditions are optimal.

Rhizomes: Iris and calla

Tuberous roots: Ranunculus and dahlia

True Bulbs: Tulip and lily

Tubers: Caladium and tuberous begonia

Corms: Crocus and gladiolus

RECOGNIZING BULBS

The term *bulb* is used to describe five types of storage organs: true bulbs, corms, rhizomes, tubers and tuberous roots. All perform the same basic function of storing food so that the plant can go dormant when conditions are too cold, dry or hot for growth. When conditions improve they sprout, using this reserve for rapid growth and flowering.

A true bulb contains a tiny stem and flower inside many layers of scale-like modified leaves. These leaves, which store food, may be tightly closed and have a protective papery covering, as on a tulip, or they may be more open and lack the papery covering, as on a lily. True bulbs tend to dry out faster than other bulbs, which are solid inside.

A corm is a compact stem with an "eye," or growth bud, at the top that elongates and produces leaves and flowers. Roots grow downward along the base. Other buds on the top or sides produce new corms.

Rhizomes are stems that grow laterally just at or below the soil surface. Buds along the top, at the tip or on the sides produce stems. Roots grow downward along the base.

Tubers are short, thick underground stems. Some are disk-shaped or have disk-shaped areas where the buds grow into stem, leaves and flowers. Roots emerge from the same area as the stems. Tubers increase in size from year to year rather than producing new tubers along the parent.

A tuberous root resembles a tuber; the dahlia and the potato are the best known of the group. Stored food makes up the bulk of the enlarged root. Buds form at one end or at eyes on the surface. Roots grow downward but emerge from all over the main root.

THE BULB LIFE CYCLE

As a bulb begins to sprout, it uses its stored food for energy. At first, the new shoots are too young and growing too fast to make much food on their own. The bulb shrinks as its food reserves are depleted by this rapid burst of growth. As leaves develop they begin to make food for growth, storing any excess in the bulb. The plant proceeds to bud and bloom. Flowering uses up a lot of food energy but the leaves are manufacturing it fast enough to allow the bulb to grow larger and form offsets, which are the beginnings of new plants.

In most true bulbs, these offsets are new bulblets on the sides of the parent. On some true bulbs new growths called bulbils grow out of the stem where the leaves attach.

In corms, the parent dies back completely, but new corms form above the old. They also develop cormels, little corms at the base of the parent.

Rhizomes multiply by growing new sections off the main stem. These sections develop into new plants complete with leaves and flower buds.

Tubers and tuberous roots simply enlarge and develop new eyes.

As the flowers fade on any bulbous plant, seeds are released. (These seeds will develop into bulbs, which may take several years to mature into flowering plants.) The leaves continue to make food and send it to the bulb for storage, but eventually these leaves also fade and dormancy sets in. The bulb and any new offsets it has produced this season now lie dormant, ready to start the cycle again when conditions are favorable.

Dormancy: Every true bulb contains a tiny but fully developed plant, which lies dormant until the right conditions trigger it to grow and bloom.

Growth: Once triggered to grow, the plant uses the food stored in the bulb for energy. Developing leaves begin to make their own food soon after they emerge from the ground.

Flowering: The blooming plant is actually at the end of its life cycle. By now the leaves are manufacturing most of the food for storage and the flower is producing seed.

Dying back: As the flowers fade, the seed ripens. At this point the leaves have finished their job and begin to wilt. The bulb has enlarged with stored food and is ready for dormancy.

11

HARDY VERSUS TENDER BULBS

THE COLD FACTOR

Many bulbs that originate in cold-winter climates will not bloom well unless exposed for a certain length of time to temperatures below 45° F. This chilling period triggers root growth that supports flowering in the spring. Without the cold, these plants usually produce a lot of weak growth and few flowers. There are also bulbs that tolerate low temperatures but do not need them in order to bloom well. *Hardy* bulbs, as they are called, grow and bloom almost anywhere. Most spring-blooming bulbs either require cold weather or tolerate it and are usually planted in the fall. This gives their roots, which begin growing almost immediately, plenty of time to develop.

By contrast, many bulbs originating in mild climates will simply die in very cold weather. Often these bulbs bloom in the summer and can be planted in the spring to grow, bloom and then die back by fall. In cold climates, dig them up before the ground freezes and store them in a cool spot protected from freezing. When the weather warms up in spring, plant them again.

Bulbs that bloom in the fall or winter can be hardy or tender depending on the variety. It is best to plant them in the spring so they have plenty of time to develop extensive roots before they bloom. After they bloom, allow hardy bulbs to die back and remain undisturbed until the next blooming season. In cold climates, dig up and store tender fall-blooming bulbs, and do not try to grow tender winter-blooming bulbs outdoors.

Crocus are among the earliest blooming bulbs. Cold does not harm them, and they often emerge right through the snow at the end of winter.

12

Bulbs Requiring Cold

Crocus
English bluebell
Foxtail lily
Glory-of-the-snow
Lily
Lily-of-the-valley
Narcissus (daffodil)
Puschkinia
Snowdrop
Squill
Tulip (most)
Windflower (some)
Winter aconite

Bulbs Intolerant of Cold

African corn lily
Amaryllis
Baboon flower
Bulbinella
Caladium
Canna
Dahlia
Freesia
Gladiolus
Glory lily
Harlequin flower
Kaffir lily
Nerine
Ranunculus
Spanish bluebell
Spider lily
Tiger flower
Tuberous begonia
Watsonia
Zephyr flower

Bulbs for All Seasons

Most bulb lovers eventually find themselves striving for year-round bulb color. In many climates this is possible. Even in climates where cool weather rules out late fall and winter flowering outdoors, bulbs can be stimulated, or forced, to bloom indoors.

Plant most summer-blooming bulbs as soon as the soil warms in the spring. Two types of lilies adorn this July garden. The same garden is shown in the small photo above featuring spring color.

Spring-blooming Bulbs Plant spring bloomers such as these daffodils in the fall.

SEASONAL CHOICES

All the plants described in the Bulb Gallery (beginning on page 54) are listed here according to their season of bloom. Keep in mind that these categories are somewhat artificial. Spring in a cold northern climate often arrives as late as May, while in a mild climate it can begin as early as February. Whatever your climate, you can enjoy months of blooming bulbs if you take a little time to plan. Many of the favorite bulbs, especially tulips and narcissus, are sold as early-, mid- or late-season bloomers. Just selecting a variety of bloom times within one type of bulb will lengthen the flowering period in your garden by months.

Be sure to mark where you plant bulbs, so you can plant new bulbs later on without disturbing those already in the ground.

Spring Bloomers
African corn lily, allium, amaryllis, baboon flower, bluebell, brodiaea, calla, camass, cape hyacinth, Chinese ground orchid, crocus, flame freesia, florist's cyclamen, foxtail lily, freesia, fritillary, glory-of-the-snow, grape hyacinth, harlequin flower, hyacinth, iris, kaffir lily, lily-of-the-valley, narcissus, ornithogalum, oxalis, puschkinia, ranunculus, spring snowflake, spring star flower, squill, tulip, watsonia, windflower, winter aconite

Summer Bloomers
Allium, belladonna lily, blackberry lily, brodiaea, caladium, canna, dahlia, gladiolus, glory lily, iris, lily, montbretia, summer snowflake, spider lily, tiger flower, tuberous begonia, watsonia, zephyr flower

Fall Bloomers
Canna, florist's cyclamen, lily, meadow saffron, nerine, spider lily, sternbergia

Winter Bloomers
Amaryllis, bulbinella, crocus, florist's cyclamen, glory-of-the-snow, kaffir lily, snowdrop, squill, winter aconite

Designing the Garden

The best way to plan a garden, whether incorporating bulbs into a mixed bed or border or planting bulbs alone, is to draw it out on paper. Think it through once you have it roughed out, and apply some of the design basics explained here for a truly pleasing effect.

Planting the Plan
Transfer the scaled dimensions from the plan to the flower bed using chalk or flour for drawing. Identify each section so you'll know where different bulbs are located.

Design Basics

There are a number of different factors to consider when planning a flower bed. Height, spacing, color, texture and time of flowering are the most important. Taken one at a time, they are quite easy to deal with.

First decide on the size and location of the flower bed. Then study the bed's exposure—how much sun it gets, how windy the spot is and how protected it is from frost and freezing. Remember that in the winter when the sun is low on the horizon it reaches under south-facing eaves but north-facing exposures are shaded. In the summer the sun is directly overhead and reaches more of the north-facing exposure but does not get under eaves or tree canopies facing south.

Once you've chosen the location and considered exposure, you can begin to choose plants and draw them onto your plan. Select plants adapted to your climate and exposure. Remember to consider the time of flowering for each bulb you pick. As you draw your plan, keep tall plants to the back of the bed and short ones to the front. If the bed will be viewed from all sides, put the tall plants in the center and work out to lower plants.

Once you have a rough sketch, you can think about color combinations, leaf texture and shape. It is especially pleasing to mix plants that have upright, sword-shaped leaves with plants that have bushy, rounded leaves. You might also consider other details such as fragrance and cutting potential. Fragrant blooms are best near windows, sitting areas, or the edges of beds or walkways where they can be enjoyed when people pass by. As you add ideas and make adjustments for your tastes and the garden's requirements, you will find that a plan begins to emerge that fills many of your needs.

Begin an all-bulb garden with a small flower bed, seen here midseason and in the photo, at left, just after planting. Expand the bed each year using the same design basics.

Companion Planting

Good Company

Though a garden with just bulbs is beautiful, especially when planned for continuous color, it can be difficult to keep it looking its best without the help of other plants. As bulbs die back they inevitably look bedraggled for a time. And in all but the mildest of climates, the fairly long dormant period for most bulbs leaves an all-bulb garden looking bare.

Almost any plant can be a companion to bulbs—even a large tree. Imagine a clump of yellow daffodils (narcissus) popping up at the base of an oak tree that has yet to leaf out. The trunk's bark sets off the bright color of the daffodils. As the flowers fade, the tree begins to sprout leaves, continuing the attractive show on its own.

More typically, bulbs are combined with annuals, perennials, ground covers and shrubs. Timing the bloom of annuals and perennials to coincide with bulb bloom can create striking garden compositions. Flowering plants also extend the show of color in a garden, which helps immensely when the bulbs are dying back.

Shrubs are great companions because they give a flower garden a sense of permanence. Some gardeners call them the "bones" or the "backbone" of a garden because they are the structure around which the rest of a garden is planned. You can use shrubs as background color or blend their foliage and flower color with that of neighboring bulbs.

Ground covers are another easy way to keep a bed of bulbs looking tidy. Plant bulbs right in the ground cover. As the bulbs begin to fade and die back, the surrounding ground cover will conceal them.

Bulbs with Shrubs
Flowering bulbs stand out well against shrubs in the background. The plants create an attractive green backdrop, and they continue to look good after the bulbs have died back. Shrubs require little maintenance compared with annuals and perennials, making them especially appealing to gardeners with limited time.

Bulbs with Annual Flowers
Besides complementing the colors in a bulb bed, annuals provide quick solutions to unexpected problems. If your bulb garden grows in a little differently than you planned or if colors are not what you imagined, a well-placed annual flower can help fill in a gap or soften clashing colors.

Bulbs with Annual Cover

Annuals in a bulb garden make good screens for dying bulb foliage. As the bulbs fade, you can plant taller annuals in front of the bulbs to hide them. You can also plant annual seeds to grow along with the bulbs. By the time the bulbs die back, the annuals will have grown high enough to conceal them.

Bulbs with Ground Cover

Ground covers create a blanket effect, and bulbs can usually grow up through them easily. As long as the bulbs grow taller than the ground cover so the blooms can be seen, the combination works well. When bulbs die back, faded foliage all but disappears into the ground cover.

Bulbs with Perennials

Because many perennials die back to the ground in the winter, they can be used in the bulb garden the way annual seed is used. Plant bulbs right behind or beside a perennial that will just be sprouting as the bulb is blooming. As the bulb fades, the perennial will be reaching full size and will hide any unsightly bulb foliage.

Bulbs to Create Interest

Because they combine well with so many plants, well-placed bulbs make valuable additions to annual or perennial gardens. For example, the up-right, pleated leaves of Chinese ground orchid add a strong vertical accent to a flower bed and often look good, even when not in bloom, from spring until late summer.

PLANTING DEPTHS & GROWING HEIGHTS

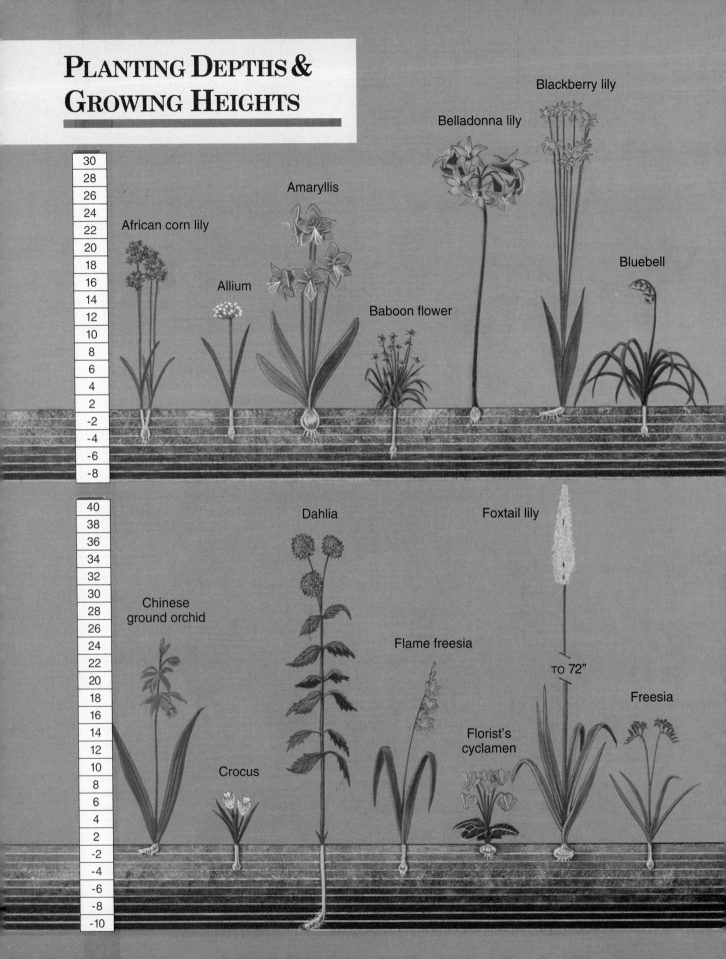

Blackberry lily

Belladonna lily

Amaryllis

African corn lily

Bluebell

Allium

Baboon flower

30
28
26
24
22
20
18
16
14
12
10
8
6
4
2
-2
-4
-6
-8

Dahlia

Foxtail lily

Chinese
ground orchid

Flame freesia

TO 72"

Freesia

Florist's
cyclamen

Crocus

40
38
36
34
32
30
28
26
24
22
20
18
16
14
12
10
8
6
4
2
-2
-4
-6
-8
-10

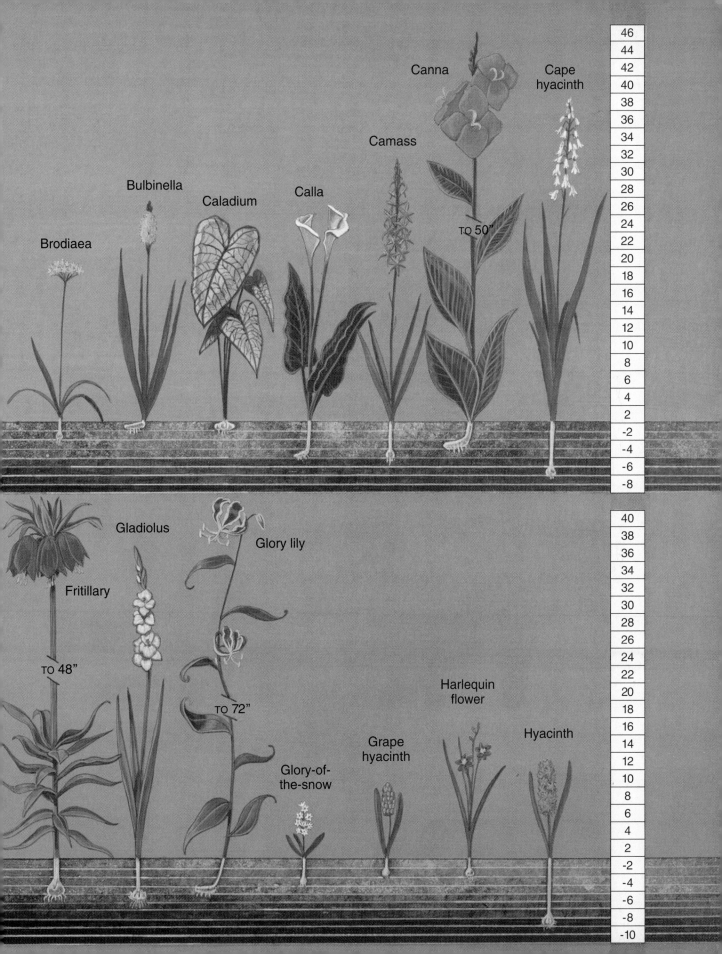

Brodiaea

Bulbinella

Caladium

Calla

Camass

Canna

TO 50"

Cape hyacinth

46
44
42
40
38
36
34
32
30
28
26
24
22
20
18
16
14
12
10
8
6
4
2
-2
-4
-6
-8

Fritillary

TO 48"

Gladiolus

Glory lily

TO 72"

Glory-of-the-snow

Grape hyacinth

Harlequin flower

Hyacinth

40
38
36
34
32
30
28
26
24
22
20
18
16
14
12
10
8
6
4
2
-2
-4
-6
-8
-10

PLANTING DEPTHS & GROWING HEIGHTS

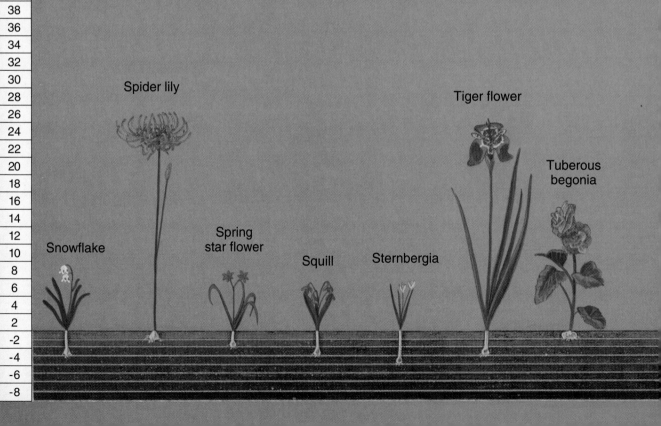

Lily

Iris

Kaffir lily

TO 48"

Montbretia

Lily-of-the-valley

Meadow saffron

30
28
26
24
22
20
18
16
14
12
10
8
6
4
2
-2
-4
-6
-8

Spider lily

Tiger flower

Tuberous begonia

Snowflake

Spring star flower

Squill

Sternbergia

40
38
36
34
32
30
28
26
24
22
20
18
16
14
12
10
8
6
4
2
-2
-4
-6
-8

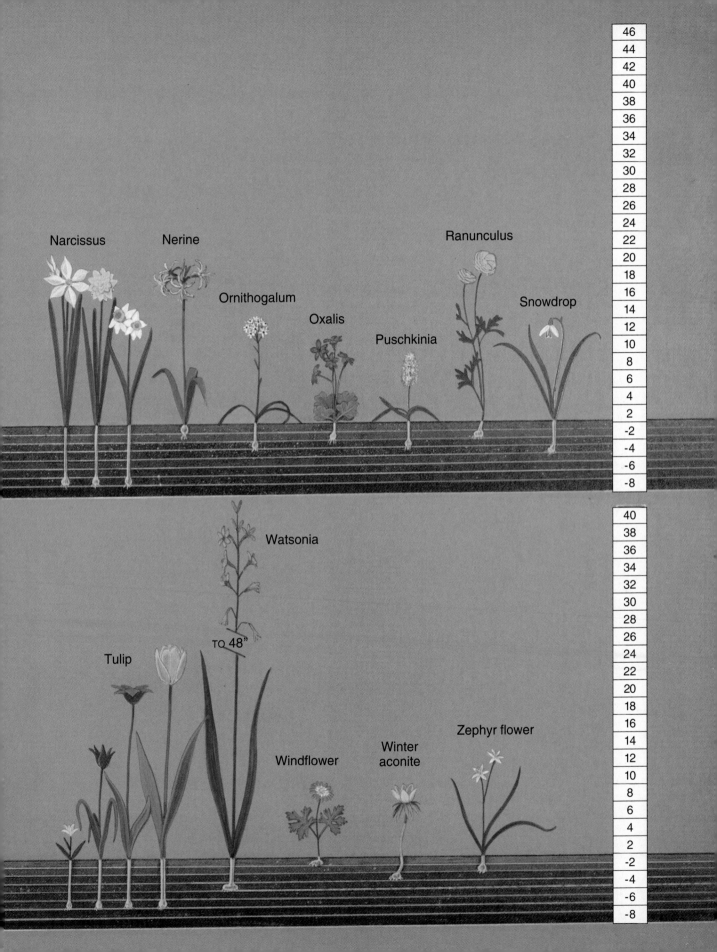

CHOOSING BULBS

Bulbs are not all the same. They vary a great deal in size and also in health, or vigor. If you know what to look for when selecting bulbs, your garden will be filled with strong plants and many attractive flowers.

Size Bulbs for any one type of plant come in various grades or sizes. A large, unblemished bulb will produce more flowers and be more likely to survive than a smaller bulb of the same type.

Disease Look for patches of gray or green mold, which signal a weak or diseased bulb. The healthy bulb on the left is dry and firm.

Damage Avoid bulbs with dents, bruises or scars. Their storage tissue is damaged, and this can weaken the plant. The blemish free bulb on the left is a good choice.

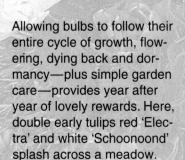

Allowing bulbs to follow their entire cycle of growth, flowering, dying back and dormancy—plus simple garden care—provides year after year of lovely rewards. Here, double early tulips red 'Electra' and white 'Schoonoord' splash across a meadow.

24

WHAT TO LOOK FOR

When you buy bulbs there are several qualities to look for. Most bulbs are graded according to size. The better the grade, the bigger the bulb, and the more flowers you will probably get from that particular bulb. The prices are higher for the larger bulbs, but the cost is justified by their superior quality. Smaller bulbs may not flower the first year, but they can be a real bargain if you want a lot of bulbs at a good price and if you have the patience to wait a year or two for the best bloom.

Always feel the bulbs before you buy them. Check them over and make sure they are firm. Moldy, bruised or diseased bulbs are fairly easy to detect and are not worth buying. And be sure the displays are well labeled so you can feel confident that you are really getting the color or variety you want.

If you are ordering bulbs from a catalog, use a reputable company. Beware of bargains that seem too good to be true. If you look around and find that the price of the bulbs is far lower than anywhere else, the quality probably is too. Bulb societies and clubs are also a good source for interesting and affordable bulbs.

Once you have the bulbs, plant them as soon as you can. If the weather is still too warm for fall planting—or too cold, if you are planting in the spring—then store the bulbs in paper or net bags. Plastic bags are airtight, and the bulbs will rot in them. Place the bulbs in a dark spot that is cool but protected from freezing. The goal of storage is to keep the bulbs from sprouting and using up their stored energy before the roots have a chance to grow.

Rot If the bulb feels soft or mushy, some type of rot has ruined the interior. The bulb on the left is firm and doesn't dent when gently pressed.

Dessication Fleshy bulbs may have dry outer leaves. These bulbs should be fat and firm. Do not buy any bulbs if they are withered or dried out.

Preparing to Plant

Good Soil

The most important step to a successful garden is to begin with good soil. The soil in most new garden beds needs some work before it is in shape for planting. First figure out what type of soil you have. To determine your soil's pH (acidity or alkalinity), you can buy a kit at the nursery and test it. Or check to see if your county Agricultural Extension office provides this service. There are also private companies that will test your soil for a fee. These tests tend to be more accurate than those done with do-it-yourself kits, and they give you more information.

You also need to know if your soil is mostly clay or sand. If your soil is sandy, water drains through it very quickly and the soil falls apart when you squeeze a handful and then open up your hand. Conversely, water soaks into clay soil slowly and if you squeeze a handful, it will hold its shape when you open your hand. Ideal soil holds its shape when you squeeze it but falls apart easily if you tap it with a finger.

All three types of soil benefit from the addition of organic matter. It loosens up clay soil, helps retain moisture and hold together sandy soil, and further enhances the structure of good soil. You can start a compost pile and make your own organic soil amendment or buy bags of ready-to-use compost.

If your soil is very acidic or alkaline, use compost to help buffer either condition. Acidic soils also benefit from applications of lime. This amendment, purchased at garden centers, lowers the acidity of soil. Alkaline soils can benefit temporarily from the addition of gypsum. Deep watering also helps by leaching out the salts that increase alkalinity.

Double-Digging

First Double-digging is a method of preparing the soil so roots grow strong and deep. Start by outlining the bulb bed with garden lime or flour.

Then Clear out any weeds or debris in the area to be planted. Cut and roll sod for disposal if the bed is in an existing lawn area.

Third Remove 8–10 in. of soil off to the side of the bed. This can be done by rows, digging one row at a time if the bed is large, or one planting hole at a time for scattered installations.

Fourth Use a garden fork to loosen the subsoil another 8–10 in. Remove any large stones you unearth.

Next Add 4–6 in. of organic amendment to the subsoil and mix it in. This provides nutrients for roots that reach this level.

Last Return the topsoil mixed with some super-phosphate and fertilizer. Rake and level the bed; water it well and allow the soil to settle for a day before planting.

Superphosphate is a fertilizer that helps the bulb roots grow well. Add it to the planting hole before placing the bulb.

PLANTING BULBS

Once the planning and designing is done and the soil is prepared, you can plant the bulbs. Use the guide on pages 20–23 for information on planting depths and bulb orientation.

Most bulbs look very effective planted in odd-numbered groups. Planting bulbs makes a good family project.

SUPERPHOSP
0-25-0

How to Plant a Bulb

First Once the soil is prepared, dig a 6–12 in. hole, depending upon the type of bulb.

Third Place the bulb in the hole—pointed end up and knob side down. Space bulbs 4–6 in. apart, depending upon the type of bulb.

Then Sprinkle superphosphate into the bottom of the hole if you have not added it to the bed yet. Follow label directions.

Last Cover the bulb with soil, tamping firmly. Water the area thoroughly. After the leaves appear, it is not necessary to water again unless the weather is dry.

YEAR-ROUND BULB CARE

Throughout the year there are a few tasks that help maintain the appearance of the flower bed and keep bulbs growing vigorously.

Marking After planting new bulbs, mark their location so that you can plant around them without inadvertently digging one up, cutting into one or planting on top of one.

Weeding Weeds compete for water and nutrients in the soil. Do your best to keep the beds weed free so the new bulbs have the best possible conditions for strong growth.

You certainly can't tell a flower from its bulb. This Darwin tulip, 'Dutch Fair,' with a bright yellow bloom stripped with orange, came from a simple brown true bulb.

Mulching A layer of mulch around plants, or over the entire bed before sprouts show, holds in moisture and inhibits weeds. Weeds that do grow up through mulch are easier to remove.

Watering Dampen the soil before installing bulbs and water well after covering the bulbs with soil. Regular watering that keeps the soil consistently moist but not soggy will encourage rapid, vigorous growth.

Staking Tall plants that tend to flop over should be staked, especially if you are in a windy area. Plants that flop to the ground get less sun and are exposed to pests and soil-borne diseases.

Fertilizing A regular application of fertilizer once the plants have sprouted increases the size and vigor of the plants and flowers. It will also help increase flower production the following year. Follow label instructions.

Deadheading When flowers fade, cut them off so the plant does not waste energy trying to make seeds. Their energy is best used to increase the bulb size.

CONTROLLING PESTS & DISEASES

Good health is the best weapon against pests and diseases. Light infestations do relatively little damage to a well-maintained plant. When the problem is severe, eradication methods may be necessary to save the bulb. Always follow label instructions when using pesticides and fungicides.

Aphids Leaves curl and distort and sometimes yellow. Often, there is a shiny, sticky substance on the leaves. You may see tiny yellow, green or dark insects. Wash them off with sharp spray from the hose. If the infestation is severe, spray with insecticide containing diazinon or malathion.

Bulb maggots (narcissus bulb fly larvae) Bulbs are soft when squeezed. They do not produce flowers, and small bumblebee-like insects appear in the spring. Buy only healthy bulbs. As a precaution, dust bulbs with trichlorfon dust before planting.

Bulb rots (fungus or bacterial disease) Bulbs are mushy and have stunted, wilting, yellowing leaves. Buy only healthy bulbs and plant them in well-drained soil. As a precaution, dip new bulbs in a solution of truban before planting. Dig up and discard infected bulbs.

Botrytis Brown spots appear that are covered with gray fuzz. Often called gray mold, botrytis affects flowers and foliage. It is difficult to control and spreads quickly. Dig up and discard diseased bulbs.

Mites Leaves have tiny spots on their surfaces and webbing on their backs. Plants grow well until heavily infested. Chemical sprays are available, but a sharp spray from the hose usually washes away mites.

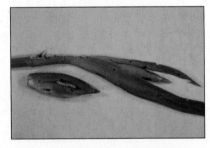

Borers Eggs hatch in the leaves of irises, and the pest bores through the plant to the bulb. Streaks in the leaves appear in spring. Keep the planted area clean of debris. Dust regularly with carbaryl, dimethoate or malathion in the spring.

Leaf spots Very small brown, gray, yellow or red spots appear and spread. Leaves may turn yellow and die. Many types of fungus cause leaf spots. Warm, damp weather encourages the problem. Discard infected leaves. Spray with copper sulfate.

Rodents Bulbs do not grow. When dug up they look chewed. Surround bulbs with chicken wire when planting to prevent gopher and squirrel damage. If mice are the problem, cover the bed with hardware cloth; remove it as shoots emerge.

Thrips Silvery streaks show up on leaves, and the tips die back. Tiny, $\frac{1}{20}$ in. long insects can sometimes be seen. Pick off infested leaves or spray the plant with acephate or carbaryl insecticides.

Powdery mildew The upper surfaces of leaves show white or gray powdery patches. Leaves yellow and die. This fungus spreads rapidly. Spray with a fungicide containing triforine. Clean up and discard diseased leaves and debris.

Slugs and snails Holes in the leaves and silvery trails on the leaves and on the ground around plants indicate the presence of these pests. Look for pests feeding at night. Remove them by hand or spread bait around the base of affected plants.

Viruses Leaves are yellow and may be streaked or mottled. Flowers may be streaked or blotched. There is no cure, but mild infections are not harmful. Remove severely infected plants and any infected lilies. Clean tools and hands after touching plants to avoid spreading the virus.

END-OF-SEASON CARE

WINDING DOWN THE GROWING SEASON

As bulb flowers fade, many gardeners are tempted to cut off the foliage in order to tidy up the garden. But the best thing you can do for your bulb plants is to continue to nurture them until they are truly finished growing for the season. The longer the leaves stay green and healthy, the longer the plant is producing and storing food for next year's growth. More food storage means more numerous and larger flowers next year.

Water and feed foliage as long as it looks good. As the leaves begin to fade and droop, water less often and discontinue feeding. Most bulbs do best if the leaves are allowed to die back completely before being removed. Then the dried, dead foliage simply pulls away. If it does not come away easily, wait a few days before trying again.

Avoid braiding or knotting spent-looking foliage; it will be less able to photosynthesize and produce food for storage. If the dying foliage really bothers you, plant some tall or bushy annuals in front of the bulbs to hide them as they die back. You can also plant a garden with perennials that will cover the foliage of spring bulbs. Many of the perennial daisies (*Chrysanthemum* species) and asters perform this function well. As the perennial plants begin to grow in the spring, they are too small to interfere with your view of the blooming bulbs. But by the time the bulbs begin to fade, the perennials have grown up enough to hide them.

Once the flowers are spent and cut away, let the greens die back to provide nourishment into the bulb for next year's growth.

Storing Tender Bulbs

First Using a garden fork, dig and lift tender bulbs from the garden before cold weather sets in. Gently shake off the soil.

Next Dust the bulbs with fungicide powder to prevent rot. Store them in a paper bag, net or old hosiery—something that allows ventilation. Do not use plastic.

Last Hang bulbs in a cool, dark, dry spot that is protected from freezing.

DIVIDING BULBS

Often after several years bulb plantings begin to look crowded and do not bloom as well as they once did. You can divide your mature bulbs to encourage vigorous growth and to increase the number of bulbs you have.

After several years, dig up and divide bulbs such as these Dutch iris. These bulbs, propagated in your garden, make great gifts.

Dividing Rhizomes and Tuberous Roots

First With a garden fork, carefully dig and lift overcrowded bearded iris rhizomes after they have stopped blooming.

Next Use a clean knife to cut them apart at narrow sections of the rhizome. Each new piece should have at least one fan of leaves.

Last Trim the leaves to 4 in. and plant the new sections just deep enough to cover the rhizome. Water thoroughly.

Dividing Other Bulbs

True Bulbs New bulbs grow to the side of the parent. Dig and lift the parent bulbs and gently break off the new ones. Replant both the original and the offspring.

Corms As the original corm dies, a new one develops above it. Little cormels may also be present along the base of the new corm. These bloom in about 2 years.

Tubers Tubers enlarge over time and can be cut up to produce several plants. Each new piece must contain at least one growing point.

LETTING BULBS NATURALIZE

THE NATURALIZED GARDEN

"Naturalized" bulbs are bulbs that grow and multiply in an open area with a minimum of care. They must be a type that is suited to your climate; that is, adapted to the minimum and maximum temperatures and the annual rainfall for your location. They are most often planted in a wild area—one that is not obviously or formally landscaped. Here they can follow their annual cycle, growing without intervention for years.

Once planted, this type of garden requires very little maintenance. An occasional feeding will speed the proliferation of the bulbs and enhance flowering, but it is not necessary. The only real work occurs when the bulbs have spread so completely that they need thinning. Even then, they will crowd themselves and naturally thin out on their own, although this process may create unwanted gaps. If you want to, dig and divide the crowded areas and replant the bulbs according to your own design.

There are only a few rules for creating a naturalized bulb landscape. First, plant in a natural pattern—which means no pattern at all. Straight lines or evenly spaced clumps do not look created by nature. A tried-and-true method is to toss the bulbs around the allotted area and plant them where they fall. This not only produces a perfectly unstructured pattern, it also ensures open, loose spacing, which allows the bulbs to multiply for many years without getting crowded. It is a good idea to place some superphosphate in the hole as you plant each bulb, just as you would in a more traditional bulb garden. And if rainfall is below average, water the area.

Naturalizing Bulbs

Allium
Belladonna lily
Brodiaea
Camass
Crocus
Fritillary
Glory-of-the-snow
Grape hyacinth
Iris reticulata
Meadow saffron
Narcissus
Ornithogalum
Snowflake
Squill
Tulip (some)
Winter aconite

Bulbs look as though they are growing wild when planted in drifts in an informal part of the yard.

BULBS FOR SHADY PLACES

Combine shade loving caladiums and tuberous begonia in containers and place them where they can be best enjoyed, such as near a shady seat.

THE SHADE GARDEN

There are a few important cultural needs in a shade garden. Shaded areas are often confined or slightly enclosed, and moisture can build up, encouraging potentially harmful fungus or disease. Adequate air circulation improves these conditions, so it's best to space plants farther apart than you would otherwise, especially if the air is very still. Shaded gardens do not dry out as fast and therefore need less water than sites in full sun. Check the soil moisture often when your shade garden is new so you can learn to apply the optimum amount of water.

Gardeners identify different degrees of shade. Deep shade is the heaviest shade. You will find deep shade between tall buildings or under the canopy of large trees.

Medium shade can be found on the north sides of buildings where it is open and bright but there is little or no direct sun. It can also be found under the canopy of trees with an open branch pattern. Only a few type of bulbs grow in this light.

Light shade is also called partial shade. It is found in bright locations that are protected from full sun by foliage or in areas that get full sun for the first part of the day only. An area that gets full sun in the afternoon is usually too hot to support a plant that needs any degree of shade.

Remember that the degree of shade a location receives may vary as trees and shrubs go through the seasons.

Recommendations for exposure refer to the amount of sun a bulb will receive when it is growing and flowering.

Shade Bulbs

Medium Shade
Blackberry lily
Bluebell
Caladium
Chinese ground orchid
Florist's cyclamen
Kaffir lily
Lily-of-the-valley
Snowflake
Tuberous begonia

Light Shade
Baboon flower
Camass
Cape hyacinth
Crocus
Freesia
Fritillary
Glory lily
Grape hyacinth
Montbretia
Narcissus
Nerine
Ornithogalum
Puschkinia
Spring star flower
Windflower
Zephyr flower

BULBS
FOR FRAGRANCE

Besides beauty, some bulbs have the added attraction of fragrance. These plants are especially desirable, and none more so than the sweet-smelling, spring-blooming bulbs that in one breath sweep away the dull pall of winter.

Fragrant Bulbs

Allium
Belladonna lily
Cape hyacinth
Crocus (some)
Freesia
Grape hyacinth
Hyacinth
Iris
Lily
Lily-of-the-valley
Narcissus (some)
Winter aconite

THE SCENTED GARDEN

Most gardeners choose fragrant bulbs for both their visual appeal and their perfume. But planting bulbs for their fragrance is a wasted effort if you cannot get close to the blossoms. For full enjoyment bring the plants indoors in pots or grow them along a walkway, under a window or near a bench.

For the most part, all would agree that fragrant flowers complement gardens and floral displays. But what smells good to one person may not to another. Most of the commonly grown bulbs that are fragrant have a very strong perfume. And generally these bulbs are chosen partly for this quality. But there are many people who find the heavy, sweet scent of hyacinth just a bit overwhelming. And paper-white narcissus, a favorite for forced indoor blooming, also seems too strong to many people. These are beautiful flowers and deserve a place in the garden—just a bit farther back if you do not appreciate their strong scent.

It is also interesting to note that although most people are able to enjoy the fragrance of freesias, there is a small percentage of the population who just cannot smell their perfume. For those few, planting freesias for their beauty alone can still be worthwhile.

Some people think that certain flowers smell better "back home," attributing this to the climate or better growing conditions. The truth is, a particular flower will smell the same no matter where it is grown; however, many plants have been bred for qualities such as color or flower size, and in the process their scent has been lost. It's important to read bulb descriptions carefully to be sure you are getting a variety that produces the flower and scent you want.

Position fragrant freesia near paths and patios where you can enjoy their visual and olfactory delights.

43

Bulbs for Cutting

How to Cut Flowers

You can extend the vase life of cut flowers by many days if you take good care of them from the start. There are several important rules to follow. The first is to cut the flowers early or late in the day but never when they are in full sun on a warm day; if it is overcast, cut them anytime. This timing ensures that the flowers are as full of water as possible. Plants lose water rapidly in the hot sun and will dry out very quickly if cut.

The next step is to immediately plunge the cut stems into a bucket of water that you have brought with you into the garden. Then take the flowers indoors and place them in a sink filled with warm water. Cut the stems again under water. This second cut is important. Plants move water up their stems through tension. When you cut the stem, a small air pocket is sucked into the stem and slowly moves up. The air pocket prevents water from moving up the stem and can bring on early wilting or cause the "neck" of the flower to bend. By immediately cutting about a half-inch off the stem under water, you cut off this bubble and avoid introducing another one. Now you can feel free to move the stems in and out of the water while you arrange them. Just try not to keep the flowers out of water for an extended period.

Many commercially available water treatments will also help preserve cut flowers. They usually come in powdered form and contain sugar to feed the plants and disinfectant to inhibit bacterial growth, which clogs the stems. These powders are mixed into the water and work well. You can make your own solution by adding about ten drops of chlorine bleach and a tablespoon of sugar to a gallon of water.

Gladiolus make stunning cut flowers in indoor arrangements. Plant part of your garden specifically for cutting; the savings between buying bulbs and buying florist flowers is considerable.

Cutting Bulbs

Allium
Dahlia
Freesia
Fritillary
Gladiolus
Hyacinth
Iris
Lily
Lily-of-the-valley
Montbretia
Narcissus
Nerine
Ornithogalum
Peruvian daffodil
Ranunculus
Snowflake
Spring star flower
Sternbergia
Tulip
Watsonia

Cut Flower Care

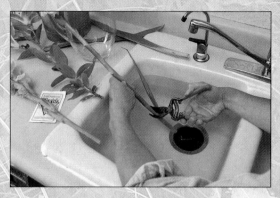

First Cut the blooms, leaving some foliage behind to provide food for the bulb. Recut the stems under warm water, removing ½ in. from the ends.

Next Select a vase and mix a flower preservative into the water. Arrange the flowers. Be especially careful with flowers that have a hollow stem; they bend and damage easily.

Last Recut the stems after about 5 days. If you did not add a preservative to the water, trim the stems and replace the water every day to extend the vase life of the flowers.

BULBS FOR OUTDOOR CONTAINERS

THE CONTAINER GARDEN

Bulbs are well suited to growing in containers. One of the great advantages of outdoor container gardening is that you do not need a yard. Just a porch, patio or balcony big enough to hold a planter allows you to grow bulbs. But even if you have plenty of space to garden, planting bulbs in containers has advantages. With container gardening, you can bring bulbs into view when they are about to bloom, enjoy their display and then move them out of sight when they begin to die back. Tender bulbs can be moved to frost-free spots during the winter. Most importantly, bulbs in pots are safe from gophers, moles and squirrels.

Plants grow especially well in containers because you can fill them with good planting soil. It is not a good idea to use soil from the garden to fill your containers, because this soil may contain weed seeds and soil-borne organisms that harm the plants. Also, garden soil often drains too slowly in a container. Containers need good drainage, so be sure there are holes in the base. Avoid small containers, six inches across or less—because these dry out very quickly.

For people with restricted mobility, planters offer a way to raise bulbs up off the ground so there is little bending and no kneeling. Place them close to the doors of your home for easy access.

Two-toned yellow daffodils, grape hyacinth and pink tulips make colorful living flower bouquets when put together in containers. Light-weight plastic pots can be moved from good growing locations to a patio or indoors when entertaining.

Container Bulbs

African corn lily
Allium
Baboon flower
Bluebell
Brodiaea
Caladium
Canna
Crocus
Florist's cyclamen
Freesia
Glory lily
Grape hyacinth
Harlequin flower
Hyacinth
Iris
Kaffir lily
Lily
Lily-of-the-valley
Narcissus
Nerine
Ornithogalum
Ranunculus
Spider lily
Spring star flower
Squill
Sternbergia
Tiger flower
Tuberous begonia
Tulip
Windflower
Zephyr flower

Planting in a Container

First If you use a hanging basket, line the inside with wet sphagnum moss. Partly fill the planter with commercial soil mix. Mix in super-phosphate according to the label directions.

Next Place the bulbs on the soil. Refer to pages 20–23 for the planting depth and correct orientation of the bulbs. Then cover them with soil.

Last Keep the planter well fertilized and well watered. Hanging baskets dry out especially quickly. Hang the planter in a spot with the proper exposure for the type of bulbs you planted.

47

THE INDOOR GARDEN

There are two categories of bulbs to grow in your home. The first includes bulbs that you can simply plant in a pot, place in a bright spot, keep watered and watch bloom. Bringing them into the house may hasten blooming, especially in winter. All they need to trigger growth is the warmth of indoors. The second category includes bulbs that require a period of cold before they will bloom. These are discussed on pages 50–51.

For indoor bloom, probably the easiest and most common bulb is fragrant paper-white narcissus. You can pot it in soil, stones or marbles, or even just set it half submerged in a vase of water. It will grow roots, send up leaves and bloom in four to six weeks. Paper-white narcissus is popular because it has a strong, sweet fragrance that has become a popular Christmas decoration for many people. The smell and sight of these spring-blooming plants in December is quite cheering.

Another very popular and easy bulb is the amaryllis. This huge bulb puts up a thick stem with blossoms up to eight inches across. Plant it in a container that is just a few inches larger around than the bulb, with the narrow neck of the bulb above the soil surface. Keep the soil evenly moist, and place the container in bright but indirect light. Amaryllis is one of the few bulbs that will bloom year after year indoors. After all the flowers have faded, cut off the stem at the base. If leaves are not already growing, they will begin to grow now. Keep the plant fed and watered until the leaves yellow, then cut them off and store the potted bulb in a cool, dark place protected from freezing. Do not water it. The following winter, bring the plant back into a bright, warm room and keep it watered. The amaryllis will bloom again.

Indoor Bulbs

Amaryllis
Caladium
Florist's cyclamen
Freesia
Glory lily
Kaffir lily
Narcissus (some)
Nerine
Ornithogalum
Tuberous begonia
Zephyr flower

Amaryllis and paper white narcissus both grow well indoors, have fabulous scents and bloom in winter, making them ideal nontraditional holiday decorations.

OUT-OF-SEASON BLOOMING

Bulbs that require a period of cold before they will flower can be stimulated to bloom by placing them in the refrigerator or outdoors for a short "winter" and then bringing them inside where it is warm for an early "spring." This process is called *forcing*.

Forced Bulbs

Brodiaea
Crocus
Dutch iris
Grape hyacinth
Hyacinth
Iris reticulata
Narcissus
Ornithogalum
Snowdrop
Squill
Tulip
Winter aconite

Combining many flowering bulbs in a container and bringing it indoors for winter color can go a long way towards chasing the clouds away. Here, tulips and hyacinth require chilling to bloom early. Narcissus, freesia and glory-of-the-snow will bloom without the need of forcing.

Forcing Bulbs

First Select healthy, unblemished bulbs from the nursery or mail-order catalog. Many are labeled "good for forcing."

Then Refrigerate the bulbs in paper bags for a minimum of 6 weeks. Do not place fruit in the refrigerator during this time—it gives off a gas that causes bulbs to sprout prematurely.

Third Use clean pots that have drainage holes. Cover the holes with pebbles or pieces of crockery.

Fourth Plant the bulbs to the correct depth in potting soil. Water them well and place the pots in a cool, bright spot.

Next When buds begin to develop, place the pots in a warm, well-lit location. Be sure to keep the soil evenly moist.

Last As flowers bloom keep them from too much dry heat or direct sunlight. Feed them with houseplant fertilizer for optimum growth, and water as needed.

BULB DATA CHART

y = yellow	b = blue
o = orange	v = violet
r = red	w = white
p = pink	c = cream
pr = purple	vg = variegated
l = lavender	g = green

NAME	HEIGHT	BLOOM TIME	COLORS	COMMENTS
African corn lily	18-24"	spring	y, o, r, p, w, c, g	Dig and store in Zones 8 and colder
Allium	6-48"	spring-summer	y, p, l, b, w	When cut, foliage smells like onions
Amaryllis	24"	spring	o, r, p, w, vg	Most often grown indoors
Baboon flower	6-12"	spring	r, pr, l, b, w, c	Dig and store in Zones 8 and colder
Belladonna lily	36"	summer	p, w	Plant just at soil surface
Blackberry lily	36"	summer	o	Red spots on iris-like flowers
Bluebell	12-20"	spring	p, b, w	Species available for all climates
Brodiaea	12-36"	spring-summer	y, pr, l, b, w	Good as cut flower
Bulbinella	24"	winter	y, c	Foliage dies down by summer
Caladium	12-36"	summer	r, p, w, g	Foliage plant; needs plenty of water
Calla lily	24"	spring-summer	w	Multiplies rapidly under good conditions
Camass	30"	spring	b, w, c	Needs moisture; tolerates wet soil
Canna	24-72"	summer-fall	y, o, r, p, w	Bold, tropical look
Cape hyacinth	24-48"	spring	w	Fragrant
Chinese ground orchid	24"	spring	l, w	Dig and store in Zones 7 and colder
Crocus	6"	fall-winter-spring	y, o, p, l, b, w, c	Often blooms right through snow
Dahlia	12-80"	summer	y, o, r, p, pr, l, v, w	Tremendous variety in shape and size
Flame freesia	10-18"	spring	y, o, r, p, w	Needs dry conditions in summer
Florist's cyclamen	8"	fall-spring	r, p, pr, l, w	Tender plant often grown indoors
Foxtail lily	3-9'	spring	y, p, w	Handle delicate roots carefully
Freesia	12"	spring	y, o, r, p, pr, l, w	Wonderful fragrance
Fritillary	12-48"	spring	y, o, r, p, w	Species vary greatly in size and color
Gladiolus	18-60"	summer	y, o, r, p, pr, l, w	Great variety of size and color
Glory lily	70"	summer	y, r	Climbs using tendrils at end of leaves
Glory-of-the-snow	6"	winter-spring	p, b, w	Tiny flower, delightful in late winter
Grape hyacinth	6-12"	spring	l, b, w	Flowers resemble bunches of grapes
Harlequin flower	8-12"	spring	y, o, r, p, pr, w	Colorful flowers; contrasting center

NAME	HEIGHT	BLOOM TIME	COLORS	COMMENTS
Hyacinth	12"	spring	y, r, p, pr, b, w	Heavy fragrance
Iris	4–50"	spring–winter	all	Immense variation within this group
Kaffir lily	24"	winter–spring	y, o, r	Tender; cannot tolerate freezing
Lily	24–60"	summer–fall	y, o, r, p, l, w	Needs some cold to bloom well
Lily-of-the-valley	6–10"	spring	p, w	Needs some cold to bloom well
Meadow saffron	6"	fall	y, p, l, v, w	Foliage appears in spring
Montbretia	36"	summer	y, o, r	Mulch in Zones 6 and 7
Narcissus	6–30"	spring	y, o, w	Vast range of color, form in bloom time
Nerine	18–24"	fall	o, r, p, w	Leaves die before flowers appear
Ornithogalum	12–24"	spring	w	Flowers have black or brown centers
Oxalis	12"	spring–summer–fall	p, pr, l	Grown for foliage
Puschkinia	6"	spring	b, w	Green stripe runs down each petal
Ranunculus	18–24"	spring	y, o, r, p, w	Amend clay soils with compost
Snowdrop	12"	winter	w	Often flowers through the snow
Snowflake	6–10"	spring–summer–fall	p, w	Good as cut flower
Spider lily	24"	summer–fall	y, r, p, w	Best in containers; some are tender
Spring star flower	6–8"	spring	b, w	Foliage smells like onions when cut
Squill	6–12"	winter–spring	p, b, v, w	Good for naturalizing; early bloomer
Sternbergia	5–9"	fall	y	Grows through winter
Tiger flower	12–30"	summer	y, o, r, p, pr, w	Flowers have contrasting spots
Tuberous begonia	12–18"	summer	y, o, r, p, w, c	Good container plant
Tulip	6–30"	spring	y, o, r, p, pr, l, w, c, g	Immense variation within this group
Watsonia	70"	spring–summer	o, r, p, l, w	Dig and store in Zones 7 and colder
Windflower	5–18"	spring	r, p, b, w	Many species to choose from
Winter aconite	8"	winter–spring	y	Good for naturalizing
Zephyr flower	12"	summer	y, p, w	Will bloom twice with plenty of water

BULB GALLERY

The plants in this gallery are listed by common name followed by their botanical name. Use the information describing each plant to select the right bulbs for your climate and exposure.

Allium
Allium species
Species of this true bulb vary in height from 6 in. to 4 ft. Most survive to Zone 4. These relatives of onion and garlic bloom in pink, lavender, blue, yellow or white in spring and summer. They need full sun and good drainage. Plant in fall. Clumps spread rapidly. *A. christophii*, which grows to Zone 7, has 6-in. clusters of lilac flowers on 12–18 in. stems.

African corn lily
Ixia maculata
In late spring, plants with long, narrow, upright leaves send up 18–24 in. stems with clusters of 2-in. flowers in colors ranging from white, cream and green to orange, yellow, pink and red, all with a darker center. Plant corms in well-drained soil, 3 in. deep in full sun. They take regular watering during growth and flowering. Dig and store corms over winter in all but Zones 9 and 10.

Amaryllis
Hippeastrum Dutch hybrids
Most often grown indoors in winter and spring (see page 48), these tender bulbs produce showy 9-in. trumpet-shaped flowers on thick, 2-ft. stems that emerge from long, strap-like leaves. Plant in pots in late fall through winter with the neck of the bulb above the soil. Place in a sunny spot. Blooms are white, pink, red, orange or bicolored. Easy and fairly quick to grow, they make a great project for children.

Baboon flower
Babiana species
Plant these corms 5 in. deep in fall or early spring in full sun to light shade for mid- to late-spring bloom. Many blue, lavender, purple, red, cream or white flowers bloom along 6–12 in. stems above fan-shaped leaves. *B. stricta* has attractive deep blue flowers on 1-ft. stems. Needs well-drained soil and regular amounts of water during the growing season. In all but Zones 9 and 10, dig and store bulbs over winter.

Blackberry lily
Belamcanda chinensis
Plant this rhizome in spring for summer blooms of red-spotted, orange-petaled, iris-like flowers on 2–4 ft. stems. Each blossom lasts 1 day, but many are produced. The vertical foliage is attractive. In autumn, mature seeds resemble blackberries. Plant just below the soil surface in full sun to light shade. It needs well-drained soil and regular watering. Grows to Zone 5 with winter mulch protection.

Belladonna lily, naked lady
Amaryllis belladonna
This true bulb comes up right after planting in late summer. Leafless 2–3 ft. stems are topped by 3–10 pink or white very fragrant trumpet-shaped blossoms. Leaves appear later. Plant in full sun with the neck of the bulb just at the soil surface. Plant deeper in cold climates. Plants are drought-tolerant and grow in any soil with good drainage. Grows to Zone 5 with winter mulch protection.

Bluebell
Endymion species
In spring, blue, white or pink bell-shaped flowers hang on stalks among long, thin leaves. Plant these true bulbs 3 in. deep in light to medium shade in the fall. *E. hispanicus,* the Spanish bluebell, is 20 in. and thrives in cold or mild climates, while *E. non-scriptus,* the fragrant English bluebell, grows to just 12 in. and does better with cold winters. They take regular watering. Grows to Zone 4 in any type of soil.

BULB GALLERY

Bulbinella
Bulbinella floribunda
Spikes of yellow or cream bell-shaped flowers top 2 ft. grassy foliage. Plant this Zones 8–10 rhizome just below the soil surface in autumn. Blossoms appear in winter. Bulbinella needs little or no water in summer, when dormant, but may benefit from light shade in the hottest climates. Plant in well-drained soil.

Brodiaea
Brodiaea, Dichelostemma and Triteleia species
Blue, purple, lavender, yellow or white flowers cluster at the top of 1–3 ft. stems with grassy foliage below. Plant corms in full sun, 2–3 in. deep in autumn. There are spring- and summer-blooming types. Hardy to Zone 6, *T. laxa*, shown here, has typical deep violet-blue flowers on 2 ft. stems.

Caladium
Caladium x *hortulanum*
The striking leaves on this 1–3 ft. tuberous plant are patterned with colorful veining and combinations of green, white, pink and red that completely overshadow the flowers. A native of South American jungles, caladium gives an exotic, tropical feel to shaded areas and indoor plantings. Plant just below the soil line in the early spring in partial sun to deep shade, and enjoy the foliage in summer. It needs rich soil and plenty of moisture. Plants are tender and must be dug up and stored over winter except in Zone 10.

Calla
Zantadeschia aethiopica
Beautiful, white, 5 in. curving flowers appear on bare
4 ft. stems above 12 in. smooth, tropical leaves. Blooms,
with their leafless stalks, make striking cut flowers. Good
drainage and plenty of moisture during bloom time are
required. Smaller hybrids in pink, rose and yellow are
available. Hardy to Zone 10, Zone 9 with mulch protection, this rhizome blooms in spring and summer.

Canna
Canna hybrids
Best known for colorful flowers and bold tropical foliage,
cannas grow 2–6 ft. in full sun, blooming in summer and
fall. White, pink, yellow, coral, apricot, orange or red
4–5 in. flowers bloom above 8–12 in. broad, flat leaves
that can be bronze, green or variegated. Dig and store
rhizomes in areas where the ground freezes in winter.
Good for boggy areas, it needs rich, moist soil and
regular watering. Grows in all zones.

Camass
Camassia species
Grasslike leaves give rise to 30-in. spikes covered with
star-shaped blue, cream or white flowers. Plant these
true bulbs in rich soil in the fall for spring bloom. Hardy
to Zone 4, camass dies back after blooming; plant near
something that will cover it. Plant in full sun to partial
shade 3–4 in. deep. It requires plenty of water. It never
needs dividing.

Cape hyacinth
Galtonia candicans
In the spring, each 2–4 ft. stem holds up to 20 fragrant,
white, bell-shaped blossoms. Thin leaves grow to 3 ft.
In the fall, plant these true bulbs 6 in. deep in full sun to
light shade. They require rich soil and plenty of water.
Hardy to Zone 5 with mulch protection. In colder climates,
dig and store the bulbs in winter.

BULB GALLERY

Crocus
Crocus species
Plant corms in autumn, 2–3 in. deep in full sun—in light shade where summers are hot. The 6-in. plants bear lavender, purple, blue, yellow, orange, cream, white or bicolored tubular flowers in spring. Choose early-, mid- and late-blooming types to extend the flowering season. Some species bloom in autumn; others bloom through the snow. They require exposure to cold and grow to Zone 3 in any well-drained soil.

Chinese ground orchid
Bletilla striata
This true orchid grows from a rhizome to 2 ft. in late spring with 3–6 lovely lavender or white blooms on bare stems. The crinkled green leaves are 12 in. and upright. In Zones 8 or warmer, plant rhizomes 1 in. deep from fall through spring in light to medium shade. Mulch in Zone 7; dig and store rhizomes in colder climates. They need rich, well-drained soil and plenty of water.

Dahlia
Dahlia hybrids
These tuberous roots produce an incredible variety of flowers in many shapes and in all colors but blue. Heights vary from 1–7 ft. In spring, plant tubers in full sun to light shade in an 8 in. deep trough. Cover with 3 in. of soil, and as the shoot grows, fill in the trough. Hardy only to Zone 8; elsewhere dig and store tubers over winter. Dahlias need well-drained soil and plenty of moisture.

Flame freesia
Tritonia species
Plant this corm 2–3 in. deep in full sun in early autumn—in spring, where winters dip below 20° F. Sword-shaped leaves grow 10–18 in. Spikes of red or orange flowers bloom in late spring. Sometimes white, pink or yellow types can be found. Dig and store corms over winter in all but Zones 8–10. This plant needs good drainage and regular watering during the growing season.

Foxtail lily
Eremurus species
In spring, *E. bungei* produces 3–4 ft. spikes of yellow flowers. *E. elwesii* and *E. himalaicus* grow to 6 ft. with pink and white blooms respectively. *E. robustus* reaches 9 ft. with pink blossoms. Plant the tuberous roots 1 in. deep in full sun in autumn. Hardy to Zone 5, foxtail lilies need exposure to cold and rich, well-drained soil. Regular watering is best.

Florist's cyclamen
Cyclamen persicum
Plant tubers just below the soil in summer or early fall in light to medium shade. Purple, lavender, pink, red or white flowers rise several inches above beautiful 8 in., heart-shaped leaves. Flowers bloom from late fall until spring. Florist's cyclamen is tender and makes a great indoor plant in Zones 6 and colder. It needs rich, well-drained soil and constant moisture.

Freesia
Freesia hybrids
In the fall in mild climates, plant corms 3 in. deep in full sun to light shade and enjoy delightfully fragrant blossoms in early spring. Plants grow to 12 in. and bloom in all colors but green. Freesias prefer mild winters and cool springs. They freeze in Zones 7 and colder but can be grown indoors in a sunny room that drops to 45° F at night. They require well-drained soil and regular watering while growing and blooming.

Gladiolus
Gladiolus x *hortulanus*
In summer, tall showy stems are lined along one side with 4-in. flowers in all colors but blue. Long-lasting fans of sword-shaped leaves are attractive in the garden. Plant corms 4–6 in. deep in full sun from fall through spring in Zones 8 and warmer. Elsewhere dig and store them through the winter and plant in spring. They require rich soil and regular watering.

Fritillary
Fritillaria species
These bulbs bloom in spring when planted 3–5 in. deep in full sun to light shade during the fall. *F. imperialis*, shown here, has whorls of red, orange or yellow bell-shaped flowers on 4-ft. stems. Other species are available. Hardy to Zone 5, they require rich, well-drained soil and regular watering while growing.

Glory lily
Gloriosa rothschildiana
Tendrils on the ends of long leaves allow this tuberous plant to climb to 6 ft. with 4-in. red-and-yellow, back-curving flowers in summer. Tender tubers survive winter outdoors in Zone 10 only. Elsewhere plant them 4 in. deep in pots in late winter and place them outdoors in full sun when frosts are past. The pots can be buried in the garden—in light shade where summers are hot. They require rich soil and regular watering.

Glory-of-the-snow
Chionodoxa species
A true bulb that blooms blue, white or pink in late winter or early spring, glory-of-the-snow is hardy to Zone 3. Plant 3 in. deep in autumn in full sun or, where summers are hot, in light shade. The 6 in. plants bear small, loose spikes of flowers that resemble hyacinths. They will naturalize in wild areas. They require rich, well-drained soil and regular watering.

Harlequin flower
Sparaxis tricolor
Late-spring flowers 2 in. across bloom in yellow, white, purple, orange, red or pink with a bright center of contrasting color. Sword-like leaves grow in fans below the 15 in. flower stems. Plant in the fall in mild climates; dig and store over winter in Zones 8 and colder. Place corms 2 in. deep in full sun. They require well-drained soil and regular watering.

Grape hyacinth
Muscari species
This early-spring-blooming bulb bears 6–12 in. stalks of true blue, pale blue or white flowers in grape-like clusters. The little, rounded, fragrant blossoms cover spikes that grow above grassy foliage. Plant bulbs 2 in. deep in early fall in full sun to light shade. Grape hyacinth is hardy to Zone 3 and requires well-drained soil and regular watering. It naturalizes quickly.

Hyacinth
Hyacinthus orientalis
Hyacinth bulbs produce strap-like leaves and in spring 12-in. spikes covered with clusters of intensely fragrant, star-shaped blossoms in purple, blue, red, pink, yellow, cream or white. Plant these true bulbs 4 in. deep in full sun in the fall. Hardy to Zone 4 when given winter mulch protection, they are great in containers or forced for indoor color and fragrance. They require rich, moist, well-drained soil.

BULB GALLERY
Iris species and hybrids

This enormously varied group of flowering bulbs includes two main subgroups: those with beards and those without. Bearded irises have hair-like tufts on their foremost, downward-hanging petal. All bearded types grow from rhizomes. Bearded irises are divided into three groups. Tall: 2–4 foot plants with showy flowers. Medium: 12–24 inches tall with large flowers. Miniature dwarf: 3–10 inches tall. Hardy to Zone 5—colder with winter protection—bearded iris blooms in all colors and many combinations.

Beardless irises grow from rhizomes or from bulbs depending on the type. Those grown from rhizomes include Japanese iris, Spuria or butterfly iris and Siberian iris. Those that grow from bulbs include reticulata iris and Dutch iris. Experts are constantly refining the divisions and definitions.

Crested iris
This category of bearded iris includes several species, all of which have a small crest at the base of each petal. The late-spring to early-summer flowers bloom in a variety of colors. Size varies from 6 in. to 2 ft. *I. tectorum*, shown here, is an unusual form with varigated leaves. Most species are tender in all but Zones 8–10; grow them in containers or dig and store the rhizomes over winter. Give them plenty of water in summer.

Dutch iris
Beardless 3–4 in. flowers on 2-ft. stems bloom in late spring in white, blue, yellow and variations of these. They make excellent cut flowers. Plant bulbs 4 in. deep in early fall. Give them full sun and plenty of water. This group is hardy to Zone 6 or colder with winter mulch.

Japanese iris
These beardless iris produce large, flat 4–12 in. purple, red, white or pink flowers on 4-ft. stems. Flowers bloom in summer and often have a contrasting edge color. Plant the rhizomes 2 in. deep in fall or spring in rich soil. Water generously during spring and early summer. They grow to Zone 5.

Siberian iris
Stems of 1–4 ft. support 2–5 blooms in blue, purple, white or pink. Plant rhizomes 1–2 in. deep in the fall. The beardless flowers bloom in spring and make good cut flowers. Give them full sun, good soil and plenty of water. They grow to Zone 4.

Reticulata iris
Hardy to Zone 6 with mulch, this beardless iris grows 4–8 in. with 2–3 in. blossoms in white, yellow, blue or purple in late winter to early spring. Plant bulbs 3–4 in. deep in good soil in late summer to early fall. They need little water in the summer after foliage dies back. This iris is good for forcing indoors.

Spuria iris
This beardless iris looks like a large yellow-and-white Dutch iris but is taller, growing on 4–6 ft. stems in late spring to early summer. Plant rhizomes 1 in. deep in the fall. It grows best in rich soil with full sun or light shade and tolerates dry summer. For the best blooms, do not dig or divide too often. It grows to Zone 4.

BULB GALLERY
Lilium species and hybrids

Lilies are extremely hardy, growing well as far north as Zone 3. In Zones 9 and 10, select only those types that do well in warmer climates. Their flowering season begins in late spring and continues through early fall, depending upon the type planted. They all flower at the top of slender upright stems, attractively clothed in narrow leaves. Lilies like a humus-rich, well-drained soil, with regular watering throughout the growing season. Give them full sun in cool areas; elsewhere, plant them in partial shade. These true bulbs should generally be planted at a depth equal to two to three times their diameter. Once the leaves turn yellow in fall, cut the stems to the ground, and mulch in the coldest areas.

Asiatic hybrids
Blooming in late spring through mid-summer, these hybrids grow 2–5 ft. with 4–6 in. flowers in white, yellow, orange, lavender, pink or red. Flowers may be upright, outward-facing or pendant. These are among the easiest lilies to grow. Plant bulbs 2–5 in. deep depending on bulb size.

Aurelian hybrids
This is a broad group of hybrids that includes trumpet- and bowl-shaped flowers. They are mostly outward-facing but include some that are pendant. This is a very colorful group with every color but blue; some white forms have green tints. Stems are 4–6 ft. and flowers appear during mid- to late summer. Plant bulbs 2–5 in. deep depending on bulb size.

Candidum hybrids
Blooming in late spring to early summer on 3–4 ft. stems, the 4–5 in. white flowers are very fragrant. Plant these bulbs in late summer with only 1 in. of soil over them. The stems will die down after flowering, and are best if allowed to dry out over the summer.

Oriental hybrids
Among the showiest of lilies, these are tall, late summer bloomers with bowl-shaped flowers or flat-faced flowers with petals that curve back. Flowers may be up to 10 in. in diameter, and are usually white with pink, crimsom or yellow centers, spots or splotches. Plant bulbs 2–5 in. deep depending on bulb size.

Longiflorum hybrids
These are the pure white Easter lilies forced in greenhouses for that holiday. The normal flowering season in the garden is mid-summer. The flowers are trumpet-shaped, and 5–7 in. long, with a strong sweet scent. The stems are 3–4 ft. Plant bulbs 2–5 in. deep depending on bulb size.

Species lilies
This is an extremely diverse group of wild lilies, varying in size, shape and color of flowers. Blooming times vary from spring to fall. Stem heights range from 2–6 ft. Many are delightfully fragrant. Planting depth depends on the size of the bulb. Tall and very fragrant *L. regale* is shown here.

BULB GALLERY

Lily-of-the-valley
Convallaria majalis
In spring, wonderfully fragrant little white or pale pink bells hang from 6–10 in. stems tucked among broad, 8 in. long leaves. Plant rhizomes in autumn, 1–2 in. deep in light to medium shade. Lily-of-the-valley must have cold winters to thrive, so it is not recommended for mild Zones 9 and 10 climates. It requires rich soil and regular watering.

Kaffir lily
Clivia miniata
Clusters of bright orange, yellow or red flowers top a thick 2-ft. stem in winter and spring. Tender kaffir lilies do not tolerate freezing; grow in pots and bring indoors for winter in all but Zone 10. The best flowering comes on old, pot-bound plants. Plant the tuberous roots just below the soil surface in plenty of organic matter. Water the plant regularly and keep it in medium shade.

Meadow saffron, autumn crocus
Colchicum species
Plant these corms 3 in. deep in summer. Star-shaped, 6 in. flowers pop up in autumn in shades of pink, lavender, violet, yellow or white. The following spring, pleated 1-in. leaves appear for a few months before dying back. Grow in any soil. They take full sun and regular amounts of water. Hardy to Zone 7.

Montbretia
Crocosmia x crocosmiiflora
Loose clumps of 3-ft. lance-shaped leaves hold 3–4 ft. zigzag stems with sprays of orange, red, bronze or yellow flowers at the ends. Plant corms 2 in. deep in spring in full sun to light shade. Montbretia blooms in summer. It is tender and needs a winter mulch to Zone 6; dig and store over winter in Zones 7 and colder. It accepts average soil and regular watering.

Ornithogalum
Ornithogalum species
Plant these bulbs 3 in. deep in early autumn in full sun to light shade for spring blooms. *O. arabicum* and *O. thyrsoides,* with black centers and brownish green centers, respectively, are 2 ft. with spikes of 2-in. white flowers and are hardy to Zone 7. *O. umbellatum,* which grows to Zone 5, spreads easily; it is 12 in. with spikes of 1-in. white flowers with green stripes. These bulbs require well-drained soil and regular watering.

Nerine
Nerine species
These fall-blooming bulbs have long, strap-shaped leaves and 18–24 in. bare stems topped with clusters of white, orange, pink or red flowers with back-curving petals. Plant the bulb with the neck above the soil surface in full sun to light shade in late summer. In Zones 8 or colder, dig and store the bulbs over winter. They require well-drained soil and regular watering.

Oxalis
Oxalis tetraphylla
A member of a large group of true bulb herbs, *O. tetraphylla,* also known as iron cross, is grown mainly for its distinct 1–2 in. leaves, which are grouped like clover. Use as a ground cover, in rock gardens or as a container plant. The 1–2 in. flowers are lilac or rose. Grows to Zone 10.

BULB GALLERY
Narcissus species and hybrids

This diverse group of bulbs commonly called daffodils or jonquils is separated into divisions. Samples of each division are shown here. All narcissi are true bulbs, and most are hardy to Zone 4. Plant them 4–6 inches deep, in full sun—or partial shade in hot climates—in fall. They grow from 6–18 inches tall, but the majority are about 12 inches tall. The center portion of the flower is referred to as the trumpet, cup or corona. Most flowers are yellow, white, orange, pink or apricot or combinations of these.

Double narcissi
This bulb group blooms in white or yellow and in combinations. Petals grow in more than 1 layer with more than 1 flower per stem. Shown here is 'Golden Ducat.'

Cyclamineus hybrids
Flowers are one per stem with back-curving petals. Colors are off-white with a pink cup, yellow with a red cup, or all yellow. Shown here is 'Peeping Tom.'

Jonquilla hybrids
Each stem bears 2–6 flowers in yellow, orange and ivory. Shown here is 'Stratosphere.'

Large-cupped narcissi
Flowers are one per stem either all white, yellow petals with yellow or orange trumpet or white petals with any color trumpet. Shown here is 'Rosy Wonder.'

Poeticus narcissi
With 1 flower per stem, its petals are white with a contrasting shallow cup often edged in red. It is very fragrant.

Tazetta hybrids
With clusters of 4–8 fragrant blooms, these are commonly called narcissus. Blooms are white with yellow or orange cups. Popular for forcing. Shown here is 'Sol d´or.'

Species narcissi
Many small and miniature types with yellow or white flowers are in this category. Shown here is *N. bulbocodium.*

Triandrus hybrids
Colors are white or yellow, or white with yellow cups. Stems bear 1–6 flowers. Shown here is 'Thalia.'

Split-corona hybrids
With mostly yellow or white flowers, these hybrids have split cups.

Trumpet narcissi
With one flower per stem, these daffodils bloom in yellow, white or bicolors. The center trumpet is as long or longer than the petals. Shown here is 'Golden Harvest.'

69

Bulb Gallery

Ranunculus
Ranunculus asiaticus
In spring, silky blossoms in white, yellow, orange, red or bright pink appear on 18–24 in. stems above attractive, low foliage. Ranunculus makes a long-lasting cut flower. In fall, plant tuberous roots in full sun—2 in. deep with the points facing down. It is hardy to Zone 8; elsewhere dig and store the roots over winter for spring planting. It needs well-drained soil. Water well at the time of planting.

Snowdrop
Galanthus species
Hanging white flowers with green markings grow on 12-in. stems in late winter in areas with cold winters down to Zone 3. Plant bulbs 3–4 in. deep in autumn in a location that gets full winter and spring sun but some shade through summer and fall. *G. elwesii,* with a lot of green on the white petals, survives milder climates. Snowdrop requires rich soil and plenty of water.

Puschkinia
Puschkinia scilloides
An early spring bulb hardy to Zone 3, puschkinia puts up 2 wide leaves and a 6-in. flower spike covered with many light blue or white flowers. Each petal has a green stripe down the center. Plant the bulbs 3 in. deep in full sun to light shade in fall. It grows best in cold winters and needs well-drained soil and regular watering.

Snowflake

Leucojum species

L. vernum, the 6–10 in. spring snowflake, and the slightly larger *L. aestivum,* the summer snowflake, have white bell flowers with green marks on each petal. They are hardy in Zones 4 to 10. *L. autumnale,* grown in Zones 4 to 10, is just 6 in. and bears pinkish blooms soon after planting in fall. Plant the bulbs 3 in. deep in light to medium shade. These plants require well-drained soil and regular watering.

Spring star flower

Ipheion uniflorum

Spring star flowers grow 6–8 in. The grassy leaves are blue-green and the same height as the blossom. Plant bulbs 2 in. deep in the fall in full sun to light shade. They are hardy to Zone 6. Flower color, depending on the cultivar, ranges from white with a bit of blue to deep blue. They do well in any soil and require regular watering while growing.

Spider lily

Lycoris species

The spider lily is closely related to the belladonna lily. Foliage dies back before the 2-ft. stems grow out to produce large white, yellow, pink or red blooms in late summer to fall. Plant bulbs just below the soil surface in late summer in a sunny spot. Hardiness varies with the species. In cold climates, plant the bulbs in containers. These plants require well-drained soil and regular watering when they are in a growing phase.

Squill

Scilla species

Flowers are white, pink, violet or blue and grow 6–12 in. Plant these bulbs 2–4 in. deep in autumn for winter to spring bloom. Squill prefers sun while flowering and light shade in summer. Species vary in hardiness: *S. peruviana* grows to just Zone 9, while *S. bifolia* grows down to Zone 3. These plants require rich, well-drained soil, and regular watering while growing.

BULB GALLERY
Tulipa species and hybrids

Tulips are a sure sign that spring has arrived. The flowers can be white, cream, yellow, orange, maroon, purple, lavender, red, pink or multi-colored. These tough bulbs are hardy down to Zone 3 and most need cold winters to bloom year after year. In Zones 9 and 10 they seldom bloom a second year; treat them like annuals. Plant 4–6 inches deep in the fall in sun or very light shade.

Mid-season tulips
This second wave of bloomers includes several hybrids. Darwin hybrid tulips such as 'Ivory Floradale,' top above, bloom earlier than their parent. The 30-in. stems hold very large blooms in vivid reds and oranges. 'Big Chief' is rosy salmon and 'General Eisenhower' is bright red. Mendel tulips, also derived from hybrids and crosses with Darwin tulips, are single and bloom in white, yellow, orange, pink or red on 20-in. stems. Triumph tulips have thicker stems, up to 20 in. long with white, yellow, red or bicolor blooms. 'Apricot Beauty,' above, is a salmon and apricot blend.

Early season tulips
These are the first tulips to appear in spring. The single types grow on 10–15 in. stems with large blossoms. They are the best types to force in pots for winter indoor color. The double flowers grow on 6–12 in. stems and reach up to 4 in. across. These can also be forced indoors. There are many cultivars to choose from, including salmon-and-orange-striped 'Princess Irene,' top above, and the fringed tulip 'Blue Heron,' above.

Late-season tulips

Darwin tulips are probably the most popular of the late-season tulips, with 20–30 in. stems and large oval blooms with square bases. Colors include white, yellow, orange, pink, lilac, purple or red. Lily-flowered tulips have narrow, pointed petals with a lily-like appearance. The long petals curve back and bloom in white, yellow, pink or red. Cottage tulips, with flowers in white, yellow, orange, pink, purple or red, resemble Darwins in size, height and oval shape. Rembrandt tulips are streaked or variegated with different colors. They are called "broken" tulips because of their coloration. Parrot tulips, top above, bloom in May and are also broken with striped or feathered petals. The petals are large and long with fringed or ruffled edges. Multistemmed tulips such as 'Orange Sorbet,' above, grow to 24 in. and bloom in white, yellow, orange or rose. There are many cultivars of each type to choose from.

Species tulips

These are good choices for mild-winter areas that do not provide the winter chilling required by most tulips. *T. fosteriana* is an early-season plant with red 4–8 in. blooms on 8–20 in. stems 'Red Emperor' is the most widely recognized cultivar. *T. kaufmanniana,* top above, is an early-season tulip with 4–8 in. stems and open, flat, pointed petals in cream to yellow with bright yellow centers and red markings on the outside. *T. turkestanica,* above, with its multi flowered stems, makes a spectacular spot planting.

BULB GALLERY

Tiger flower, Mexican shell flower
Tigridia pavonia
This true bulb blooms in summer and has lance-shaped, pleated leaves up to 18 in. long. The 3-petaled flowers grow up to 6 in. across, and each 12–30 in. stem carries many blooms in purple, red, orange, pink, yellow or white. Plant in full sun to light shade 2–4 in. deep in spring. Tiger flower is hardy to Zone 7; elsewhere dig and store bulbs over winter. It requires well-drained soil and regular watering while growing.

Sternbergia
Sternbergia lutea
Bright yellow, crocus-like blooms appear atop 5–9 in. stems in early fall. Foliage grows through winter and dies back in spring. Plant bulbs 4 in. deep in mid to late summer. Sternbergia is hardy to Zone 6 if given winter protection. It needs full sun and well-drained soil. Water regularly while the plant is growing.

Tuberous begonia
Begonia x *tuberhybrida*
Tremendous variety in both flower color and shape characterizes these showy summer-blooming 12–18 in. plants. Colors range from red, orange, yellow, pink, and cream to white. Place tubers just below the soil surface in light to medium shade in spring when frost is past. Begonias must be dug and stored over winter except in Zone 10. They require rich, moist soil.

Watsonia, bugle lily

Watsonia species

These spring and summer bloomers grow up to 6 ft. with double rows of white, apricot, red, salmon, pink or lavender flowers. Plant corms 4 in. deep in full sun in fall in mild climates. These plants are hardy to Zone 8. In Zones 7 and colder, plant in the spring; dig and store the bulbs over winter. They grow in any soil and need regular watering while growing.

Winter aconite

Eranthis hyemalis

Sweet-smelling, cup-shaped, butter yellow flowers grow to 8 in. in late winter to early spring. Hardy to Zone 4, winter aconite needs cold to do well. Plant tubers 3 in. deep in fall in a spot with winter and spring sun but a bit of summer shade, preferably under deciduous trees or shrubs. It needs rich, moist, well-drained soil.

Windflower

Anemone blanda, A. coronaria

Plant tubers in fall or spring in full sun to light shade for spring bloom. *A. blanda* is a white, pink, rose or blue daisy-like flower on an 8-in. stem that thrives to Zone 6. *A. coronaria,* shown here, the poppy anemone, with larger, poppy-like flowers blooms in blue, white, red or pink, grows to 18 in. and thrives to Zone 7. It needs rich, well-drained soil. Keep soil dry through the summer.

Zephyr flower, fairy lily

Zephyranthes species

Late-summer blossoms of white, yellow or pink grow to 12 in. above grassy foliage. Plant bulbs 1–2 in. deep in early fall in full sun to light shade. Plants may bloom more than once in mild climates if allowed to dry out and then watered again regularly. In Zones 8 and colder, plant in the spring and dig and store bulbs over winter. Zephyr flower needs well-drained soil and regular water.

PLANTING ZONE MAP

HOW TO USE THIS MAP

The map outlines eleven zones in North America for the purpose of determining plant hardiness. It is based on the United States Department of Agriculture's figures for minimum winter temperatures.

It's important to understand that the zones are designed to provide basic information, not absolute parameters.

You may, for example, live very near a zone border or in a microclimate such as a sunny, south-facing valley. If that's the case, you may have slightly higher temperatures more like those in the next warmer zone. Or perhaps you're near the highest elevation of your region in a windy spot with temperatures more like the next cooler zone.

Good winter protection will extend the life of your bulbs in marginal zones where plants may be in danger during the coldest months. Use a protective layer of mulch—such as leaves, evergreen boughs or straw—over the plants. The colder it is or the less hardy the plant, the more mulch you need. Use a foot or more if you're in Zone 3 or cooler or are in the coldest recommended zone for a particular plant. Fall mulching helps keep crowns from freezing and thawing repeatedly.

On the other hand, you may live where heat is the source of potential damage to your bulbs. Shade from arbors or trees will help keep afternoon sun from damaging plants. Regular watering and a moisture-saving layer of mulch on the soil also help.

Watching and working with nature is part of the excitement and challenge gardening offers. Whether it's adapting to nature's sometimes harsh conditions or reveling in the beauty of a single flower, true satisfaction comes from the ongoing process of making the garden the best it can be.

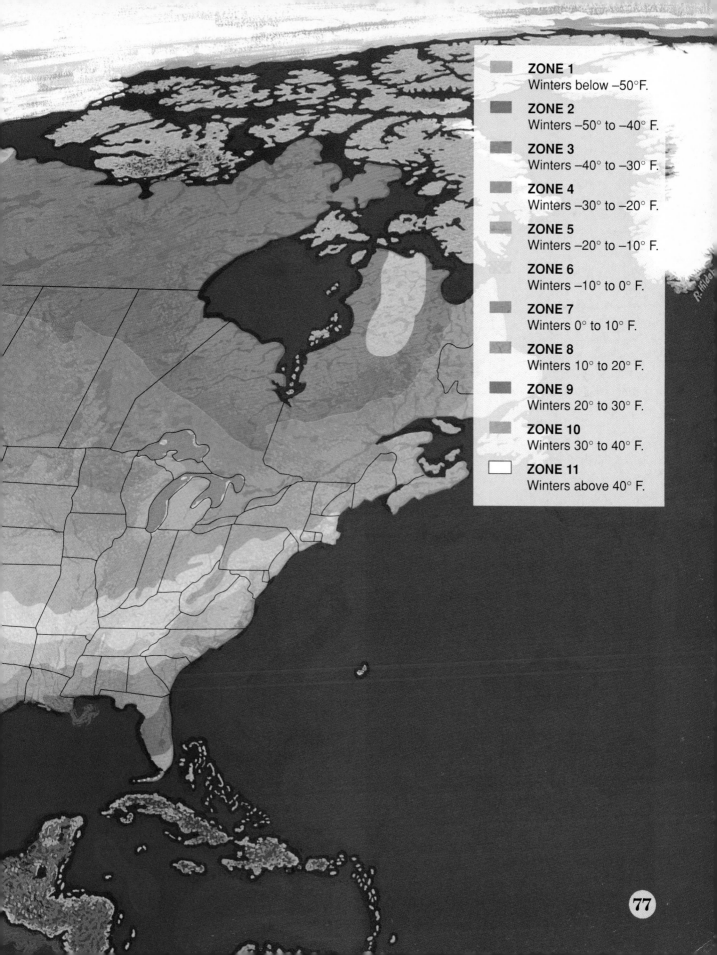

ZONE 1
Winters below −50°F.

ZONE 2
Winters −50° to −40° F.

ZONE 3
Winters −40° to −30° F.

ZONE 4
Winters −30° to −20° F.

ZONE 5
Winters −20° to −10° F.

ZONE 6
Winters −10° to 0° F.

ZONE 7
Winters 0° to 10° F.

ZONE 8
Winters 10° to 20° F.

ZONE 9
Winters 20° to 30° F.

ZONE 10
Winters 30° to 40° F.

ZONE 11
Winters above 40° F.

INDEX

A NOTE FROM NK LAWN & GARDEN CO.

For more than 100 years, since its founding in Minneapolis, Minnesota, NK Lawn & Garden has provided gardeners with the finest quality seed and other garden products.

We doubt that our leaders, Jesse E. Northrup and Preston King, would recognize their seed company today, but gardeners everywhere in the United States still rely on NK Lawn & Garden's knowledge and experience at planting time.

We are pleased to be able to share this practical experience with you through this ongoing series of easy-to-use gardening books.

Here you'll find hundreds of years of gardening experience distilled into easy-to-understand text and step-by-step pictures. Every popular gardening subject is included.

As you use the information in these books, we hope you'll also try our lawn and garden products. They're available at your local garden retailer.

There's nothing more satisfying than a successful, beautiful garden. There's something special about the color of blooming flowers and the flavor of home-grown garden vegetables.

We understand how special you feel about growing things—and NK Lawn & Garden feels the same way, too. After all, we've been a friend to gardeners everywhere since 1884.